N... g from c... ifficulty ... ks up a ... elations ... s fellow ... nd perpetual disbe...

Married, with two children, he is the author of three textbooks on communications and has also written several items for TV and radio comedy shows – mostly dreamed up while dodging the wheels of 30-ton juggernauts and 90-mph company reps on the A12 near his home in Colchester.

Derek Chambers now takes the train from his home in Hockley, Essex, to work in London, where he is a partner in a design consultancy firm. He has decided that driving does not suit his profession – the drawing board kept getting in the way of the steering wheel. His previous activities, which allowed plenty of scope for driving, included travelling round the world as a photographer on assignment for 'Newsweek' magazine. He is married with a daughter and two sons, all of whom are hell-bent on beating their father's impressive record for collecting parking fines.

Also in Arrow by Michael Bland

A PIG AT THE WHEEL

A Bigger Pig at the Wheel

Michael Bland

Illustrations by Derek Chambers

ARROW BOOKS

To Thomas and Ben

Arrow Books Limited
17–21 Conway Street, London W1P 6JD

An imprint of the Hutchinson Publishing Group

London Melbourne Sydney Auckland
Johannesburg and agencies throughout
the world

First published by Arrow 1984

Set in Linoterm Memphis
by JH Graphics Limited, Reading

Printed and bound in Great Britain
by Anchor Brendon Limited, Tiptree, Essex

ISBN 0 09 936150 7

CONTENTS

WHY A BIGGER PIG?

Being a successful road-hog is hard work. And it's getting harder. Every day 7,000 new cars are registered and an even bigger stream of cars and lorries pours onto the roads – **your** roads. It's impossible to enjoy driving on them because of all these morons wandering around the place with no clue where they are going or what they are doing.

Worse still, some of them have read 'A Pig at the Wheel' and learnt the techniques of making everyone else's life a misery on the roads, and others are copying their nasty habits. There's only one thing for it. You must become an **advanced** road-hog . . . a **bigger** Pig at the Wheel.

Hence this essential guide. By studying the enemy in detail you can learn to anticipate his or her next move and stay a step ahead. By learning techniques like the 'double-start', the 'non-indicating right turn' and 'follow-my-leader', you can once again enjoy the simple pleasures of hogging the road while others shout, flash, hoot and shake their fists.

Most important, you will be taught the mental approach to being an advanced roadpig – how to develop a state of mind in which you are naturally pig-headed, bad-tempered and inconsiderate the whole time so that the techniques come naturally. For this we must understand what makes a roadpig. What is it, deep in our natures, that turns us from normal, polite civilized human beings into raving lunatics the minute we get inside a car and turn the ignition?

First there's the sense of **possession**. It's **your** car. You're very proud of it and it cost a lot of money. Everything else on the road is a threat to your beloved status symbol.

Secondly there's the **frustration.** All you want to do is to go from one place to another, and if the roads were empty it would be quite a pleasant experience. But all you ever get is traffic jams, roadworks, lorries, crossroads, traffic lights, and thousands of idiots getting in the way.

Thirdly you feel **protected** because you don't have eyeball-to-eyeball contact. When in the presence of other people we tend not to spend our time mouthing obscenities at them, shaking

our fists and making rude signs. We have a sense of politeness and social conduct which restrains our in-built aggression. Besides, we might get thumped. Safe in our four-wheeled suits of armour, however, we are removed and protected from our fellow human beings and feel free to give vent to our natural unpleasantness.

Lastly – and this is what it's **really** all about – there's our **caveman instinct.** Back in primeval times we were always on the move and always watching the others out of the corners of our little piggy eyes. The first one there would get the best cave, while the last one would make a tasty take-away dinner for a sabre-toothed tiger.

So to this day we always feel uneasy and **competitive** when we're going anywhere. Not just in cars. When we're walking along a busy street and come up behind someone who's going slower we become totally preoccupied with getting past. We jostle and shove and quicken our step, and will often end up walking at twice the speed at which we started. And when we're driving we can't bear to get stuck behind someone who's travelling at one mile an hour slower than us. It's almost as bad as being overtaken.

There's only one thing for it. Get into training now. Learn the techniques in this book and develop an attitude of mind which makes you automatically meaner than the rest of them. Become a **bigger** Pig at the Wheel.

THE ENEMY IN MORE DETAIL

In 'A Pig at the Wheel' we took a brief look at some of the creatures with whom we have to share the roads. Off-putting wasn't it? Yet to succeed as an **advanced** roadpig you will have to study the weird habits of the strange beings who dare to occupy your road space. Only then can you learn to outwit them and do unto them as they would unto you.

So grit your teeth and read on . . .

Pedestrians

It seems incredible that someone should want to go anywhere without a car when the good Lord has given us two perfectly healthy legs to operate a clutch and accelerator, yet large numbers of people actually seem to **enjoy** the slow and unaccustomed act of walking. It's best

to adopt an air of smug superiority and try to ignore these inferior creatures, but some of them take on the motorist on his own territory and need careful watching. For example:

Jaywalker

So named after the sporting bird which is difficult to 'bag' because of its cocky manner and quick reflexes. Great patience is needed to lure this bird into coming one step too close so that you can add it to your tally. Not to be confused with:

Streetwalker

Also noted for its gay plumage and audacity. Shares its habitat with the **Common Kerb-crawler.** Both can be considerable distractions to the roadpig, whose only idea of 'forbidden pleasure' is carving up a Panda car on the Hanger Lane Gyratory System.

Edge-of-pavement artist

This is the breed of pedestrian which hovers on the edge of the pavement as if about to step out into the road just as you drive past. The commonest variety is the **Doddering Old Dear**, which can be identified by its distracting habit of looking the wrong way while one foot dangles over the kerb.

Jogger

A relative newcomer to these shores, the **Jogger Bird** is already a prolific pest. Recognizable by its bright 'jogging suit' plumage which it changes each Christmas, it believes that because it is jogging it is entitled to use up an entire lane and not move over for cars. Despite sterling extermination work by roadpigs and truck drivers, this species is on the increase and can often be seen in pairs and, occasionally, large groups.

Hitch-hiker

For the male roadpig this is a bird which usually turns out to be a bloke. A slender figure, tight jeans and long blonde hair can make the road-pig forget that he was about to turn off at the next village. Only after you have stopped and asked 'How far do you want to go?' do you spot the beard and piece of cardboard with BRADFORD scrawled on it.

Watch out, too, for the species of male hitch-hiker which plants its attractive mate as a bait and hides behind a nearby bush with their half ton of wet rucksacks.

Picking up hitch-hikers is an act of generosity completely alien to the natural meanness of the average roadpig, but if you ever do feel a sudden philanthropic urge towards one of these creatures take great care. For a start, hitch-hikers always stand where you can't stop – 20 yards after a busy roundabout, for example. Having stopped, you will then be unable to pull out again because of all the traffic pouring past. And there are two other types to watch out for: those whose travels of the last two months have not taken them in the vicinity of a bath, and those who are so lonely from their travels that they have six weeks' worth of talking to catch up on.

Pedestrian herds

Sometimes the unwary roadpig is intimidated by creatures on foot banding together and blocking the road. They may even cause you the ultimate indignity of making you stop altogether.

The most civilized variety are herds of cows or sheep. Farmers always find it necessary to move the brutes down a narrow country lane when you are in the maximum hurry. Some roadpigs try to nudge their way through, which is all right if you don't mind hoof prints on your bonnet.

The human equivalents are **Peace Marches** (about which there is nothing remotely peaceful) and **Fun Runs** (in which no-one seems to

be having any fun). These, too, are carefully planned to coincide with your most urgent journey of the year.

Pedestrians may even create impromptu herds, for instance when you are trying to get out of a side road into a busy shopping street.

Cyclists

Cyclists are nothing more than pedestrians on two wheels, but they are able to louse up the roadpig's enjoyment of an otherwise uncluttered road. Most frustrating are the disgustingly healthy tourists – usually from Scandinavia – who scorch along at a speed just too fast to overtake in comfort. The skimpy shorts above the racing saddles are filled to overflowing with bulbous bottoms and the pedals are pounded by legs that make King Kong look like an underweight stork. These migrants generally travel in pairs and the male is the one with the hairiest legs. If both sets of legs are equally hairy the male is the one in front.

The commonest domestic variety is the traditional **Old Codger**, recognizable by its tobacco-stained moustache, tattered raincoat and complete lack of any impedimenta such as lights or brakes. Known for its distinctive wobble, especially after leaving its second home at the Dog and Ferret, this breed of cyclist has a charming unpredictability which makes even the most determined roadpig stand by for avoiding action.

Motorcyclists

A common form of motorcyclist is the **Young Nerk** – a younger version of the **Great Yobbo.** This youthful creature can be seen overtaking lines of busy traffic on the wrong side of the white line, sitting astride a 200 cc sewing machine with an L plate and no silencer. Few survive to adulthood, but those that do survive metamorphose into a **Great Yobbo** by shedding the L plate, growing a larger engine and wearing a studded jacket.

A favourite trick of the **Great Yobbo** is to open its throttle in your blind spot while you are negotiating a roundabout or trying to overtake a meandering caravan. There is nothing more unnerving than hearing a deafening roar from somewhere behind, but not knowing if it is overtaking on the inside or the outside – or jumping over the top of you.

But no motorcycling daredevil can match the courage of the **Lesser Jemimah Puddleduck**, a diminutive biped wearing an enormous white crash helmet and perched precariously on a putt-putting little scooter at 20 mph. The sight of one of these gallant creatures happily occupying the centre of its lane, oblivious to the fuming juggernaut two inches behind it, is enough to stir the heart of the dedicated roadpig.

So much for the lesser beings. We now move on to the roadpig's main competition – other motorists. There are many different types and it is important to know their distinguishing features.

Cars

The car-driving types to watch out for are:

Company reps

Reps are issued with cars which achieve the impossible. Any normal person driving a basic 1.6-litre car finds it hard to accelerate from 60 to 110 in top gear up a steady incline. So if you're driving up the motorway with all three litres at full revs and an innocent-looking family car comes hurtling past like a dingbat with diarrhoea, you know it's a company rep at the wheel.

To confirm the sighting, look for the telltale jacket hanging neatly on a coathanger by the nearside rear window. The repmobile will often be an estate version packed with cardboard boxes full of unmentionable things.

At least the company rep tends to keep himself to himself and steers well clear of other road-users, unlike the:

Boy racer

The Boy Racer is easily identified by the fourth-hand 'sports' version of a standard saloon with several useless accoutrements to make it look

like something beastly, e.g. racing decals, stick-on spoiler, an aerial the size of the Eiffel Tower and enough fog lamps and driving lights to light up Liverpool v. Real Madrid in extra time.

The Boy Racer's characteristic behaviour is to appear in your mirror at a closing speed of Mach III when you are driving perfectly sensibly along a winding road. It then tries to unnerve you by swerving violently from side to side – looking as if it will overtake on the inside if it can't get past on the outside – and finally roars past in second gear at the narrowest point of a blind bend and sets off in pursuit of another victim.

This 'tailgating' action is not to be confused with that of the more friendly:

Social type

This is the gregarious sort of driver who comes up behind you and then stays there whatever you do to shake him or her off. If you speed up **he** speeds up. Slow down and **he** slows down. Nor does it help if you turn off and take a different road. The Social Type tends to fall in love with the car in front and follow it faithfully wherever it leads him.

If, however, the vehicle which appears from behind and dogs you is a white car with blue lights on top it is not one of the friendly Social Type. This is the less friendly **Ello-Ello-Ello Bird** – which only appears on the scene when you haven't been watching your speedo or your tax disc has expired.

Weekend driver

The Weekend Driver, or **Common Twit**, is a species which emerges only between 5.00 pm on Friday night and midnight on Sunday. Its sole aim is to make life hell for the motorist who simply wants to get from A to B along his usual road and at a reasonable speed.

The first type you encounter at a weekend is the **Friday Night Specialist** whose natural habitat is the centre of a large town. Its weekly migration to nowhere-in-particular is timed to coincide with the evening rush hour. After blocking up all the roads out of town this creature can be found wandering along the trunk roads of Britain with a mile-long stream of traffic behind it. Those on dual-carriageways and motorways can be seen meandering from lane to lane, windows steamed up and the passengers pointing in all directions at once while the driver tries to read the map, look at its watch, argue with its mate – and occasionally steer the car. In summer the addition of a caravan doubles the **Friday Night Specialist's** ability to bring the nation's traffic to a fist-shaking standstill.

The next day its close relative, the **Saturday Morning Specialist**, ambles out of its lair to wreak havoc on anyone with a legitimate reason for being on the roads.

And on Sunday the king of the weekenders, the **Sunday Doodlebug**, ventures forth to take the air. The morning is spent wheeling the family chariot out of the garage – where it has sat all week – and lovingly cleaning and polishing it. After lunch the family are herded in, the yellow duster is put on the dashboard, and the nylon pile cushions are placed conspicuously on the back shelf.

Then it's hey-ho for the open road. A master roadpig in its own right, the **Sunday Doodlebug** potters happily along the country lanes, its engine never going over 2,000 rpm, blissfully unaware of road signs and white lines and unconscious of the existence of anyone else on the roads.

It is not certain where this species goes to during its outing as no-one has ever had the patience to follow one, but it can often be seen in tearooms, country parks and on boating lakes, resting between bouts of driving. For the most part though, it just seems to wander around aimlessly until the evening, when it's time to give the faithful velocipede a quick rub-down and put it back in its stable.

Shoppers on wheels

The **Shopper Bird** is noted for its erratic, darting action as it travels along searching for supplies. Its small estate car is only let out for weekly shopping trips, so there is no need to use the mirror or indicators. Its characteristic behaviour is to stop without warning or nip unpredictably in and out of parking spaces (or **any** spaces) when it spots tasty morsels in shop windows.

Holidaymakers

The warm weather brings flocks of this migrant out onto the roads. Its random wanderings are enhanced by the large numbers of things floating around in the back – such as suitcases, dogs and children. Visibility is further hampered by holiday-camp stickers and ends of rope dangling from the overladen roof rack.

It is advisable to keep well clear of a **Holidaymaker** during this annual ritual as it has a disconcerting habit known as 'Signpost Fixation'. Every time it sees a signpost it will suddenly go into a trance, sometimes causing it to stop and shoot off unpredictably in any conceivable (and often inconceivable) direction.

Knight riders

The opposite of the **Holidaymaker**, this high-speed beast knows exactly where it is going. The driver, belonging to the **Stinking Rich Smoothie** variety, hurtles past lesser beings with a brutish snarl from five litres of engine and a row of gleaming silver exhaust pipes. Although its machine costs more than a small hotel, the **Knight Rider** is unable to go on holiday as there isn't enough room inside for a pyjama bag, let alone a suitcase.

DIY type

This remarkable breed of road-user spends the majority of its time underneath the bonnet rather than in the car itself. It derives more pleasure from bolting, banging and welding than from the simple delights of hogging the road. If not tinkering in the garage it can be found scavenging for big ends on scrap heaps. When making a rare foray onto the public highway the **DIY Type** is distinguishable by the clouds of smoke pouring out of its exhaust pipe and the loud knocking noise from the engine.

Taxis

There are many types of taxi, the main ones being the **London Cab** and its **Country Cousin.** The London variety spends its life driving round looking for pedestrians, though it is never sure which it prefers – picking them up or mowing them down. Careful study has shown that so long as the pedestrian stands still and waves an arm gently the taxi will be friendly and pick it up. But it will pounce on any moving biped, particularly when trying to cross the road.

London Taxis are noted for their yellow lamps. These are lit by candles – which is why they go out the moment it starts to rain.

But the real fun of taxi travel starts when you arrive at a remote country station and phone for a cab. Half an hour later a clapped-out, 10-year-old heap coughs and splutters up to the station and limps to a halt in front of you. As you look sympathetically at this expired wreck you realize with horror that it is, in fact, your transport, and the only alternative to being ferried in this old bone-shaker is to walk. The one consolation is that if you actually reach your destination the fare will cost only a fraction of the London equivalent.

The 'driving-for-40-years-and-never had-an-accident' bird

So named after its familiar and often repeated cry, this harmless-looking creature is actually one of the deadliest on the road and should be avoided at all costs. Watch out for the telltale signs: flat tweed cap, string-backed gloves and several badges on the front to show how competent and experienced the driver is. The reason it hasn't had an accident in 40 years is that it has been too busy **causing** them with its bloody-mindedness and insistence on its rights.

Lorries

Though all the roadpig's natural enemies make life miserable, lorries do have a certain something extra: they tend to come off best in an

argument. There is a point at which other road-users, however determined, may waver at the last moment to avoid damage to his or her most prized possession. Even the **Been-driving-for-40-years-etc. Bird** will occasionally brake or swerve if it knows it's in the wrong (never if it believes it's in the right), but to a steaming great truck the merits of the case don't really matter.

Actually, lorries are much friendlier and more likable than people realize. For example:

THEY ARE GENEROUS
– on a rainy day a lorry will kindly give your car a high-pressure wash when you try to overtake. As part of the service it will pay particular attention to spraying your windscreen to keep it nice and clean for you.

– they are more than happy to share some of their load with you. Chains, bits of metal and containers full of interesting chemicals are dispensed onto the roads with magnanimity. Lorries are also fond of leaving shredded tyres on the motorway (and presumably driving on without them as you only ever see the tyre and not the lorry who lost it).

– sometimes a lorry will go through a ritual called 'load shedding' in which it generously shares **all** of its timber, glass or oil drums with the other road-users.

THEY ARE PLAYFUL
– lorries love a friendly race. No matter how fast

your car, a lorry will gladly give you a burn-up whenever you want one (or don't want one).

– another of its favourite games is to creep up on an unsuspecting motorist half asleep in a traffic jam and release the air pressure from the brakes just behind his left ear. Much fun is had by all as the victim jumps out of his skin and looks round in terror for the source of alarm.

– sometimes when the mood takes them (usually on roundabouts in the rush hour) a lorry will playfully roll over to have its tummy tickled.

Lorry types

They come in all shapes and sizes. Some of the most popular are:

All cab and no lorry

Cabs can get very frustrated sitting around in a garage all day with no load to pull around so they are sometimes let out on their own for exercise. Free of their 20-ton containers, these cabs frisk and romp along the highway, letting off steam in a flat-out sprint.

Glass carriers

These strange-looking creatures with high, tapering sides look as though they would blow over in the first puff of wind. Along the sides are large frames with vicious brackets sticking out like the scythes on Boadicea's chariot wheels. Ostensibly the brackets are for carrying large panes of glass, but in reality they are fitted to deter would-be overtakers. This is why you never actually see them carrying any glass.

Sand and gravel lorries

By contrast, these are deceptively wide beasts which crawl painfully through congested towns and along busy trunk roads at peak periods. The load is so burdensome that they try to lose most of it on the road between the quarry and their destination by pouring it through the gap beneath the tailboard.

Incredible hulks

It is a stirring sight to see one of these double trailers, the size of a couple of slag heaps on wheels, thundering through the night. Indecipherable hieroglyphics on the side and the number plate show that it comes from some Central European State adjacent to the one where the vampires come from. Even if you were to survive an argument with one of these brutes, you certainly wouldn't survive one with the driver, who is built like a gorilla and sits in his cab, 20 feet above the road, gripping the steering wheel with great hairy arms the width of telegraph poles.

Mobile acid baths

As a guaranteed means of keeping other road-users at a respectful distance, some lorries carry ominous tanks bearing orange signs, exclamation marks and a skull and crossbones, warning of the destruction of the entire earth inside five minutes if they leak or anyone lights a match.

Strange creatures of the night

On the road, as in the jungle, everything changes at night. A different breed of creatures, shy and sinister, takes over. Skulking shapes lurk in the hedgerows and on the kerb, their eyes reflecting in your headlights. Most terrifying of all, some strange beings with eerie, luminous reflectors take to the roads to scare the living night-lights out of even the most hardened road-pig.

The humble jogger, for example, becomes a startling distraction. All the driver sees at first is an intermittent flashing from the roadside. A leprechaun lighthouse, perhaps? A stroboscopic cat? On closer inspection it turns out to be a pair of reflective running shoes, apparently jogging along on their own.

Some cyclists, too, strike back at the motorist with reflectors on their pedals and by sprouting a paddle-like apparatus which sticks out to the side and makes the bike look twice its actual size.

But the most fearsome phantom of all at night is a rider in reflective clothing on a black horse. As you innocently round a bend on a dark country road you are suddenly confronted by a headless body, suspended six feet in the air, jogging gently up and down.

The roads at night are no place for the faint of heart.

A BIGGER PIG ON THE ROAD

If you have studied the Basic Roadcraft section in 'A Pig at the Wheel' you are now ready to learn some **really** basic roadcraft. To be one up on the other roadpigs you must learn to outdo them at their own game. You must practise all their moronic, aggressive, petulant, stupid, arrogant, belligerent and incompetent habits – only worse.

As with the martial arts, the true master of the road is the one who develops the right **mental** approach. Having learnt the physical disciplines – such as a suitably aggressive driving position, Variable Speed Driving, non-indicating and

pig-headed parking – you are ready to learn the mental disciplines needed to be a complete pig without having to think about it. The art of Zen Roadpiggery.

So, before turning the key in the ignition, sit for a moment in the calm of your garage or the car park and reflect on the journey ahead. Think of the opportunities for making everyone else's life a misery. Picture yourself carving up commuters, lousing up lorries, petrifying pedestrians, terrifying taxi drivers and generally making a complete pig of yourself. By being in the right state of mental preparation you will find that all the bloody-minded and inept techniques described in this chapter come instinctively.

Recite the ten golden rules of pig driving to yourself again and again until they become second nature:

1. I am the only person with a right to be on the road.
2. I am the only person who knows the first thing about driving.
3. I will not look in the mirror.
4. I will not use my indicators – unless it is to confuse others.
5. I will not be overtaken.
6. I will use up as many parking spaces as possible.
7. I will not know where I am going until I get there.
8. I will let myself be distracted by as many things as possible.

9. My two most treasured attributes are my horn and my headlamp flasher.
10. At all times my next action will be a complete mystery to all other road-users – and to myself.

This, presumably, is what driving instructors mean when they talk about **anticipation.** Even before you start up, look around to see what discomfort and inconvenience you can cause to others. Is anyone nearby having a conversation which you can drown with lots of noisy revving? How much of the atmosphere can you poison by running your engine for a few minutes? Above all, is some unsuspecting person standing behind your exhaust pipe – a spouse in a new dress or suit happily loading the boot? If so, switch on at once and listen with glee to the anguished yells from behind the car.

Now, do you remember your pulling-out drill?

1. Pull out.
2. Look in your mirror (a rare exception to Rule 3) at the car standing on its nose behind you.
3. Indicate to let him know you have pulled out.

Good. But now add some of that **mental** discipline to your driving and **think ahead**. When pulling out onto the main road, wait until there is a car coming – or better still a whole stream of traffic – and pull out in front of it. Remember that a hallmark of a good roadpig is to remain unscathed, so don't cut it too fine. Just enough to be a nuisance.

Having ruined your victim's enjoyment of an uncluttered road and made him have to think about getting past you, you should now potter along, well out into the road, exuding plenty of smelly smoke from your exhaust. The next stage is to look for an opportunity to leave him stranded – by nipping through the next traffic lights just before they change, for example, or overtaking a lumbering great lorry and disappearing over the horizon just before the oncoming traffic stops the car behind from overtaking too. This will give you the pleasure of knowing that your victim is sitting there fuming because if **you** hadn't carved him up **he** would have got past the lorry and be miles down the road where **you** are now.

A variation on the theme is to pull out in front of a car(s) as above, forcing it to slow down, and then turn right, making him sit there behind you mouthing obscenities while you wait five minutes for a gap.

Thus by adopting the right sort of mental approach to your driving you can ruin some other road-user's day within minutes of starting out on your journey.

Be unpredictable

With practice you can gradually develop a perpetual state of studied unpredictability at all times – but you have to work at it. Nothing is more guaranteed to wind up your fellow motorists. If they don't know what on earth you're going to do next they have to keep their distance, worry and, above all, **concentrate** – an alien activity which ruins their own enjoyment of ambling along the road in a mental vacuum.

The master of unpredictability is our friend the

Weekend Driver, and it is well worth studying this creature's habits . . . preferably from a distance. Watch, for example, how he puts into practice the Variable Speed Driving techniques described in 'The Road-hog's Guide' – crawling round the bends, speeding up on the straights so no-one can overtake . . . the fellow is an inspiration.

Having mastered some starting up and pulling out procedures it's time to try your hand at the highly advanced **double start** and unpredictable **right turn.**

Double start

Can be done at traffic lights and road junctions, but best at roundabouts. Stop before entering the roundabout and wait until a car has pulled up behind you. Now rev, grip the steering wheel anxiously and, as soon as a gap appears, accelerate rapidly. Then change your mind and stop. The driver behind, assuming you have gone, will be busily looking to his right to see if the way is clear. By the time he looks round he is already charging towards your stationary rear end. Try if possible to move away again as soon as he has screeched to a stop, leaving him stranded on the roundabout.

Right turn

In the basic manual we learned how to turn left into a side road at the last moment without indicating – to the exasperation of the driver waiting to pull out onto the main road. The more advanced **right** turn demands perfect timing, positioning and the use of the indicator. So you will need to practise. In particular, try and work out which one is the indicator switch.

Wait until some poor fool is waiting to conduct a right turn out of a side road on the right. Look as though you are going straight ahead so that he cannot get out.

Once he is waiting submissively for you to go past, slow down gradually so that he doesn't know what on earth you are going to do next.

Then, when it is impossible for him to get out in front of you, start to indicate and watch the apoplexy on his face.

DO NOT LEAVE ROOM FOR ANYONE BEHIND YOU TO OVERTAKE ON THE INSIDE. That way a nice long queue of traffic will build up behind you. Finally, you sedately drive round across his bows and leave him sitting there chewing the steering wheel in frustration for five minutes while the traffic clears.

Constructive dithering

Dithering comes as second nature to the Weekend Driver. But you may have to work at it. The art of successful dithering is to never be sure about **anything**. Don't make your mind up about a course of action until the last minute and then, once you've made it up, change it.

Line-of-traffic techniques

A good example of the constructive dither is the 'I've just realized I want to overtake him after all' tactic. This is employed when you have been peacefully following another car for miles and a faster car comes up behind and wants to overtake. Suddenly the old competitive spirit is kindled and you position yourself half outside the car in front so that the newcomer can't get past either of you. Wander back in occasionally to raise his hopes then, as soon as he starts to make his move, change your mind and pull out again. It's important not to be seen to have noticed the car behind. Make him assume that you are blissfully unaware of his presence (which, indeed, you may be). See how long you can keep this up before actually overtaking – or not overtaking – as the mood takes you.

If you're in a line of traffic and really can't be bothered with all this dithering in and out, be sure to drive with your bumper half an inch from the exhaust pipe in front of you to prevent anyone from overtaking and cutting in.

Another important technique is 'Follow-my-

Leader' which is used when your line of vehicles comes across an obstruction such as a parked car or lorry in your path. If the leader pulls out into the opposite lane to get past then it is of course safe for the following car to do likewise, and the next, and the next . . . The oncoming car with the right of way just has to sit there and curse.

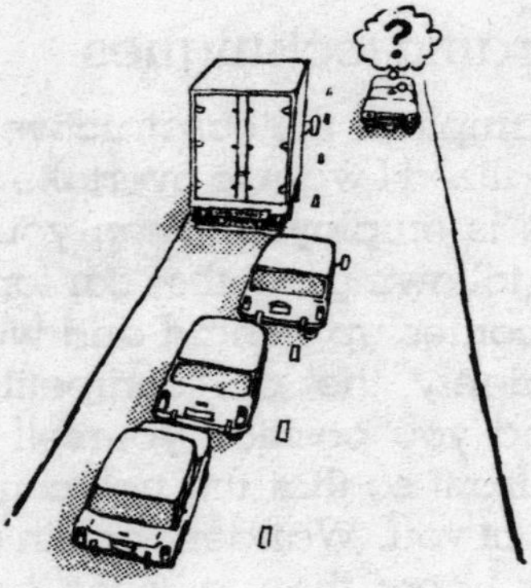

For the advanced roadpig: If you are the car being forced to wait while they all invade your territory one after the other, the counter is to creep imperceptibly forward until one of them gets stuck because there isn't enough room to squeeze through. You can then sit there holding up all the oncoming traffic, unable to go anywhere yourself but smugly satisfied that you are in the right.

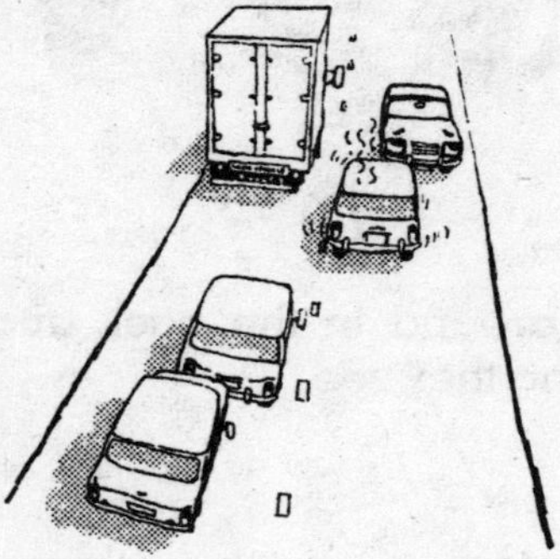

Distractions

It is sometimes tempting, particularly on a long journey, to lose your concentration on being a roadpig and to start thinking instead about your driving. This undesirable trait can be resisted by surrounding yourself with distractions, for example:

Animals

- outside the car, such as a cat running across the road, or
- inside the car, e.g. a small pack of yappy dogs

rushing around in the back and barking at everything they see.

Kids

– also yapping at everything they see, fighting, arguing, having to stop to empty little bladders and – always at **the** most inconvenient possible moment – 'Daddy, I'm going to be sick'.

Passengers

– as well as the famous **Back Seat Driver** there's the **Ohjustlookatthatlovelyhouse Bird** who delights in drawing your attention to every feature in sight, and the **Lecher Bird** with its familiar cry of 'Corgetaloadofthatyoudon'tget-manyofthosetothepound'.

Windscreen washers

– these should be set so that when you press the button a jet of water squirts over the top of your roof and sprays the windscreen of the baffled driver in the car behind.

Electronic gadgetry

– modern cars come with wonderful built-in distractions such as trip computers, warning lights, alarm buzzers and funny little voices telling you that your oil pressure has dropped. By the time you've interpreted the orange light with the wavy lines on, calculated how many miles you're doing to the gallon, set the digital clock and worked out how to stop that damned voice telling you that your oil pressure is too low you find that you've got from A to B without actually looking through the windscreen.

Cigarettes

– smoking while driving provides a number of useful distractions. Having a cigarette in the steering-wheel hand while changing gear gives you practically no control over the wheel, and keeping one in your mouth means that you can hardly see a thing for the acrid column of smoke spiralling up your nostrils and past your eyes. Regular smoking also ensures that your windscreen has a permanent yellow film of slimy tar all over it and the inside of the car has ash flying everywhere whenever you open the windows or put the fan on. The best distractions though, are when you open a new packet or dispose of a fag end. There's no way you can open a cigarette packet without using both hands, so the hapless driver behind sees you suddenly start to veer all over the road for no apparent reason. Then the cellophane wrapper comes fluttering out of the window, followed by the foil wrapper. Sometimes an empty packet will come bouncing along the road. But the highlight comes when you discard the still-burning cigarette end, especially at night when you can scare the following motorist out of his wits as he sees this mysterious fireball come snaking towards him.

Road Signs

– you were warned in 'A Pig at the Wheel' that road signs are guaranteed to spoil the fun of driving – especially if you try to work out what they mean. Some are delightfully pictorial and start the imagination working overtime.

What, for example, would a man from Mars make of this?

Eventually our visiting Martians will deduce that they have stumbled on the practice ground of the great Evil Knievel.

Or this one?

Strange creatures, those earthmen. Their outside toilets have no walls.

And the natives are decidedly hostile. Sometimes they push rocks over the cliff at you:

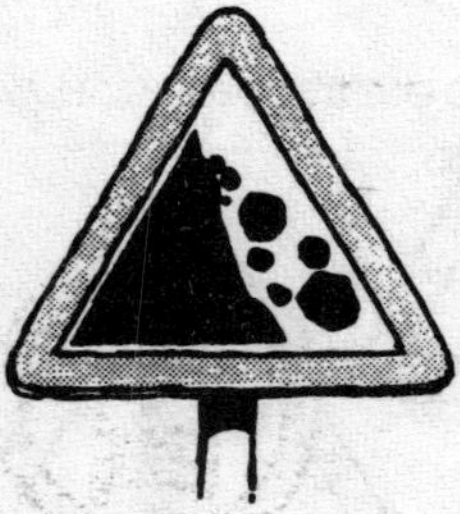

And sometimes they attack with bayonets:

or they invoke the wrath of their gods:

They put up signs telling of powerful aphrodisiacs:

and leave others blank for people to make whatever they want of them:

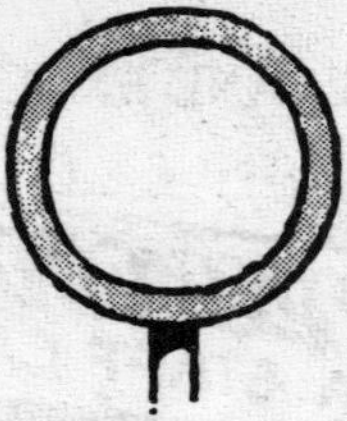

But at least they have a sense of humour and enjoy a good laugh:

Stickers

– a sticker or two in your rear window makes an ideal distraction for other drivers. For a moment they forget about the important business of overtaking you and close in to read the miniscule lettering. The psychology of car stickers is fascinating. They are meant to be a sign of individuality – yet they almost all look the same, say the same, and are unreadable from half a bonnet's length. Here, for the sticker buff who has always wondered what they said but didn't like to ask, is a collection of some of the more amusing ones:

WARNINGS AND EXHORTATIONS

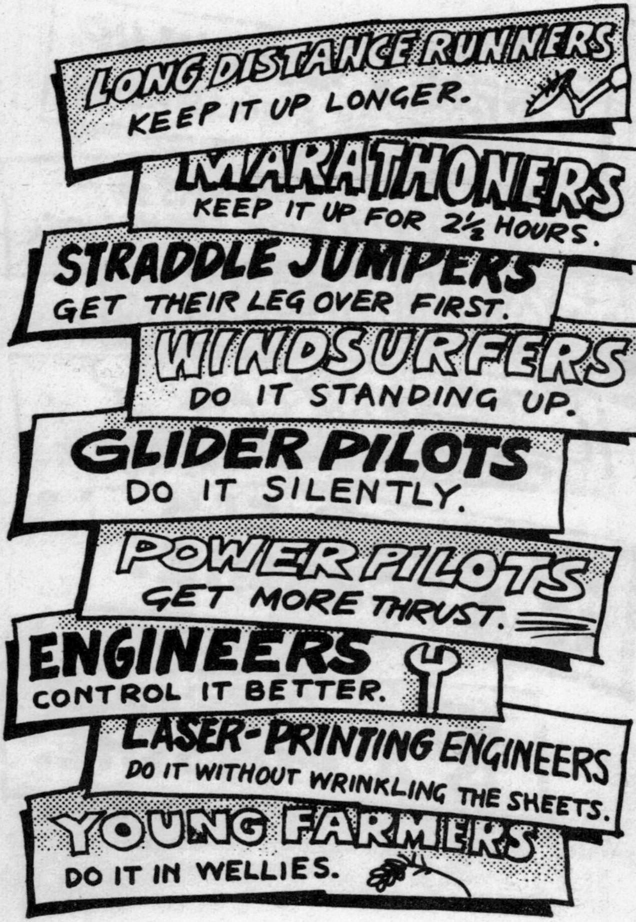
LONG DISTANCE RUNNERS
KEEP IT UP LONGER.
MARATHONERS
KEEP IT UP FOR 2½ HOURS.
STRADDLE JUMPERS
GET THEIR LEG OVER FIRST.
WINDSURFERS
DO IT STANDING UP.
GLIDER PILOTS
DO IT SILENTLY.
POWER PILOTS
GET MORE THRUST.
ENGINEERS
CONTROL IT BETTER.
LASER-PRINTING ENGINEERS
DO IT WITHOUT WRINKLING THE SHEETS.
YOUNG FARMERS
DO IT IN WELLIES.

INFERIORITY COMPLEX

Seen in the rear window of a Porsche 924.

Route finding

The best way of taking your mind off your driving altogether is trying to find your way when you don't know where you are, where you've been and where exactly it is that you're going.

This performance starts with the person you are visiting saying 'Don't worry, you can't miss it', followed by you reminding your partner, kids, dogs, cat and luggage as you pile them all into the car, that you have an incredible sense of direction, are an expert map reader, never get lost and know the road like the back of your hand.

At first all goes well. You are on familiar ground and know the name of the town you are going to and roughly which county it is in. All you have to do is to go cross-country to the M something-or-other, turn off at Junction 15 (or is it 17?) follow the signs for Mazechester, and then take the A417862 until you see the sign for Little Grunting just before the pub after you've passed a fruit farm on the left. Couldn't be easier.

You would think that if you head off in the general direction of a motorway you will eventually reach it, motorways being quite large targets. But roads have a subtle habit of starting out in one direction and gradually wandering off in another.

Then you come to a T-junction where both directions are at a right angle to the one you want to go in. And there are no signs to the motorway. After exploring the country lanes of old England for a while you do not notice that the bridge you've just gone under was, in fact, the motorway. You press on.

Eventually you trace your way back to the motorway and discover that the point where your road crosses it on the map is not an intersection after all. The nearest junction is 10 miles in the wrong direction. By now you've worked out that it was Junction 16 you wanted, so you duly turn off at said junction and arrive at a road which goes over the motorway. The sign tells you of two different towns depending which direction you take . . . neither of them Mazechester. There is no-one around to stop and ask.

Finally, you find the road to Mazechester and your troubles are over – until you come to a large roundabout with dozens of roads leading off it. The big **green** road sign half a mile before the roundabout said Mazechester on it, but you didn't have time to see which of the umpteen exits you had to take. But when you reach the roundabout there is only a complicated-looking **white** road sign with roads leading to Boggins-in-the-Marsh, the station, a town centre but you don't know which town, and an industrial estate. The latter is particularly bad news as industrial estates are nowhere near the towns to which they belong.

After a few circuits of the roundabout, a tour of the industrial estate and a quick look round the town centre, you spot a passing peasant and ask for directions. Little Grunting is easy to find, he says. You go through the first lights and right at the second ones by a garage. Go on for three

quarters of a mile and take the first proper turning to the right; up a hill and half left at the third roundabout; keep going until you pass a bus station, then look for the signs to Great Burping . . .

It's amazing how time flies when you're enjoying yourself. You haven't given a thought to your driving all morning and you can look forward to the fact that after lunch you have to reverse the whole procedure.

Flashing

Flashing your headlamps means whatever you want it to. If, for example, you are driving along in the **outside** lane of a dual-carriageway and someone ahead of you in the **inside** lane wants to pull out to overtake a slower vehicle . . . give him a quick flash. By this you may mean:

> 'Come on; I'll let you out', or
> 'Stay there; I'm coming through'

. . . or anything else for that matter.

If he starts to pull **out** you will, of course, have meant your flash as a warning for him to stay **in**, so you are entitled to much annoyance, honking and more flashing.

On the other hand, if he thinks you have flashed to tell him to stay put then you should sit just behind and outside him, impatiently drumming your fingers and wondering why the fool can't understand a simple signal and get on with it.

Flashing can be utterly confusing in a busy street when an oncoming car is waiting for you to come through before he can pull out round a parked vehicle.

Your quick flash of the headlamps tells him, of course, that you are going to carry on and he must watch out. At this point the moron pulls out into your path because he mistook you to mean 'come on'. He then has to negotiate his way back while you drive through, glaring in righteous indignation.

Conversely, you might occasionally be feeling

magnanimous and decide to let him through. Although it's patently obvious that your flash means you'll wait for him, for some incomprehensible reason he thinks you are telling him to wait. So you both sit there looking at each other. You flash again to repeat your message. He's not sure and still sits there. You decide that this is all getting a bit silly so you engage gear and start to go through – just at the moment that he decides you meant 'come on' and starts to come through too . . .

With practice you can move on to the more advanced technique of meaning all things to all people – such as when one car is waiting to come towards you and another is trying to get out of a side road.

At this stage you flash the oncoming car to tell him he can come through. Or you flash the one in the side road to let **him** know **he** can come out. Or both – it doesn't really matter. Either way, each driver thinks you are only flashing at **him** as he hasn't seen the other one. So they both pull out at the same moment . . .

Motorway driving

For the advanced roadpig, motorways present a whole new challenge. There are new ways of demonstrating your unpredictability, intolerance, stupidity and total incompetence. You might think that two or three wide lanes of straight motorway would simplify things and reduce the opportunities for making life miserable for your fellow motorists. But fear not. We have our methods.

The first point to remember is that there is no such thing as three lanes. The inside lane is only for the use of others and it is your duty as an advanced roadpig to stay resolutely in the middle lane – except when the mood takes you and you feel like pottering along in the **outside** lane for a while.

The only time to stick to the **inside** lane is when someone is trying to join the motorway from a slip road:

Though perfectly possible for you to move out into the empty outside lanes and let this interloper in, it would be an unthinkable act of consideration. You have the right of way and must assert yourself by crawling steadfastly along and making him wait. Once past the slip road you should return to your customary position in the middle lane.

You can apply the same principle when already in the middle lane and a car on the inside lane is waiting to overtake a lorry:

But you, too, have decided to overtake the lorry at some time in the next 10 miles. The fact that you are only going a tiny bit faster is neither here nor there – and there's certainly no reason why you should move out into the outside lane just because it's empty. As for that impatient idiot on your inside . . . he can wait till you've finished your performance.

Sometimes you will find yourself in the outside lane after overtaking something and may decide to return to the middle lane where you feel most comfortable. This feeling should in no way be influenced by the long stream of exasperated cars behind who, for reasons known only to themselves, seem to want to get past you. In these circumstances try to resist any temptation to pull over promptly and decisively. Half a mile in front of you is another vehicle which you may or may not want to overtake in due course, and if you move back into the centre lane you will have to go through all the agony of pulling out into the outside lane when you get there.

So stay put for a while before deciding that maybe you would prefer to be back in the dear old middle lane after all. Then start to wander back so that the cars behind you think they can finally slip past you and get on with their journey. Well, maybe you'd better stay in the outside lane. Or maybe not. By wandering half in and out you can occupy the entire motorway for mile after mile.

One way to relieve the boredom of motorway driving is to single out a motorist who is happily driving along at a safe, steady speed, minding his own business, enjoying the weather and concentrating on his driving. The first he sees of you is when you go flying past him in the outside lane. He will ignore this lunatic and carry on enjoying his journey, little realizing what you have in store for him.

Now, once past him, pull back into his lane and decide that you have no reason to hurry after all and are going to relax and enjoy the scenery. Gradually you slow down so that the car you've just overtaken finds himself closing on you and has to slow down too. His pleasure is slightly marred by the presence of your rear end, especially as you need a re-bore and lots of nasty, smelly fumes are pouring out of your exhaust.

Frustrated, he indicates, pulls out and overtakes. While he is doing so you imperceptibly speed up so that by the time he returns to his lane he is travelling at 5 miles an hour more than he was originally.

At this point you suddenly remember that you really had better be getting along a bit, so you speed up and go hurtling past him again. Before long your mild-mannered little motorist is foaming at the mouth, his eyes glaring demoniacally, and he is tearing down the outside lane at 100.

Bad weather driving

There's nothing like a spot of bad weather to bring the advanced roadpig into his own. You will have to work hard at it as everyone else drives stupidly in adverse conditions, too.

Rain

Rainy weather is highly prized by the motoring world. You can see this from the way that the moment it starts to rain everyone takes to the roads.

In **towns** the advanced roadpig drives at half his normal speed when it's raining. This causes huge tailbacks and makes everyone late for work. But on the **open road** he doesn't let the rain make any difference. The presence of three inches of water on the road and the fact that he can't see through his windscreen do not deter him from zooming along at his usual speed, driving too close to the car in front and generally being his usual impatient, pig-like self.

Wind

Similarly, no notice is taken of a trifle like a Force 10 sidewind which keeps pushing the car off the road.

Fog

If driving in thick fog an advanced roadpig tries to get to his destination as quickly as possible before it gets any worse. He becomes mesmerized by the stuff so that he doesn't have a clue what speed he's driving at and is blissfully unaware of what might be going on around him. So long as he can't see what's happening in front there's obviously nothing to worry about.

Ice

One feature of ice is that it often can't be seen, which must mean, of course, that there's nothing to be afraid of. In fact, even if there **is** a black sheet of the stuff all over the road it doesn't feel all that different, so the advanced roadpig will just keep tanking along at his usual pace until there's a need to stop. He then brakes sharply.

Snow

While a good roadpig enjoys driving in rain, wind, fog and ice as if they weren't there, a few flakes of snow throw him into an instant panic. His aim then is to drive so slowly that he comes to a stop and can't get started again. He stays in the lowest possible gear, with maximum revs, and on arriving at a hill always stops at the bottom before attempting to slither up in first gear with the engine screaming and the wheels spinning uselessly round.

A pig at the pump

Filling up with petrol is an inconvenience. But for the advanced roadpig it can have its compensations. Some people actually enjoy standing there in a howling gale watching their money flashing past on the readout. With a little practice, though, you can soon spoil their simple pleasure.

On arrival at the filling station, quickly size up the situation and see if you can grab someone else's pump. If another motorist is negotiating to place his car so that the filler hole is nearest the pump, nip in quick and snatch his place . . . and then look to see which side of the car **your** filler hole is on.

Your aim when filling up should be to prevent as many people as possible from getting their petrol until you have finished. This means taking up as many pump spaces as you can. By stopping far enough in front of – or behind – your pump you can stop anyone from getting in to the one next to you. And be sure to stop at the first pump you come to so as to prevent people from getting through to the empty pumps beyond. If you park far enough away from your pump you can block the gangway on both sides.

Then increase their frustration by spending hours filling up, fumbling with the filler cap and taking ages to pay.

Courting

The trouble with cars for courting in is that they are cramped, the seats are the wrong shape and they don't have curtains. Not recommended for the advanced roadpig, who by now should enjoy the finer things of life – such as polishing the car or doing battle with a stream of Sunday morning motorists.

However, if you **must** use your car for courting the best method is as follows:

Make sure that your partner is nice and relaxed after a good meal and a few drinks – and check that her seat belt is done up. Put some soft, dreamy music on the cassette player, chat her up, run your fingers gently through her hair and, when the moment is right, ask her if she wants to make love to you.

If she says yes, use the car to drive straight down to Brighton for a dirty weekend.

A PIG ABOUT TOWN

The advantage of a town is that it brings large numbers of vehicles – all of them in a hurry and all going in different directions – into one small area. With only a little thoughtlessness and stupidity you can shred the nerves of the most patient motorist, block up entire streets and create a veritable orgy of flashing and honking.

For many a roadpig London, with its high-speed bustle and welter of one-way streets, is the Mecca. Here you can drive round all day getting hopelessly lost, changing your mind, dithering, dicing with taxis, getting stuck in bus lanes, turning in traffic jams, hooting, swearing, swerving and generally enjoying yourself.

Before graduating to such dizzy heights, however, it is advisable to practise your town driving techniques in less ambitious surroundings.

For a start you must overcome the urge to concentrate. With so many other vehicles tearing around in close proximity it's tempting to start thinking about what you are doing and watching where you are going.

Do try to switch off and relax. Turn the radio on full blast and snuggle up to the car in front, thinking about whatever happens to come into your head. Every now and then the car you are following will stop suddenly for some reason

beyond comprehension and you will notice at the last second that he is, in fact, stationary. Slam on your brakes so as to stop half an inch from his bumper – with much squealing of brakes. Since the cars behind you have also been driving along with their drivers' minds in neutral you will hear a succession of last-second tyre screechings until, from half a dozen cars back, there comes a dull thud and the tinkling of glass as one extra switched-off driver is caught out.

The one exception to driving around in a permanent trance is when waiting to pull away at a traffic lights when there are two or more lanes and you have other motorists on either side who have the audacity to want to pull away first. In these circumstances engage gear and sit there with one foot on the clutch and the other on the accelerator. Rev noisily for the two or three minutes that the lights are at red then, the moment they turn to amber, release the clutch.

On the occasions when you don't (a) stall, (b) find you were in third gear or (c) find you were in reverse, your car will hurtle forward and you can take the lead. Keep accelerating for a quarter of a mile, when you will have to stop at another set of traffic lights which have just turned red – and all the other cars in the race will join you again.

So you wait with your clutch in and your engine revving, lights change, roar off, take the lead, quarter of a mile, more traffic lights, red, stop, joined by others . . . you can never say that driving through town is dull.

Remember your lanesmanship, too. Try to occupy as many lanes as you can and keep wandering from one lane to the other as the mood takes you. But watch out for the dreaded 'Two's Company, Three's a Crowd' situation where three lanes suddenly become two. It is not recommended to be the roadpiggy in the middle.

A great challenge for the **advanced** roadpig, though, is that of taking up the whole of a road which is single carriageway but wide enough for two lanes. The idiots in front and behind you may make two lanes of it, but this is no reason why **you** should, so be sure to position yourself in such a way that you can't be overtaken on either side. Ideally, get behind another vehicle and look as if you are going to overtake it – without actually doing so:

Blocking techniques

Driving in town presents the skilful roadpig with unlimited opportunities for bringing everyone around him to a standstill. It can be highly satisfying to sit and look at a row of cars which can't get anywhere, their engines overheating and drivers at boiling point, and knowing with smug satisfaction that it's all your doing. As you develop your blocking techniques you can learn how to bring a whole street to a standstill or, with a bit of luck, an entire town.

Don't be overambitious at first. Practise on a few pedestrians. Once you have mastered the art of splitting up a crowd of shoppers trying to cross a side road:

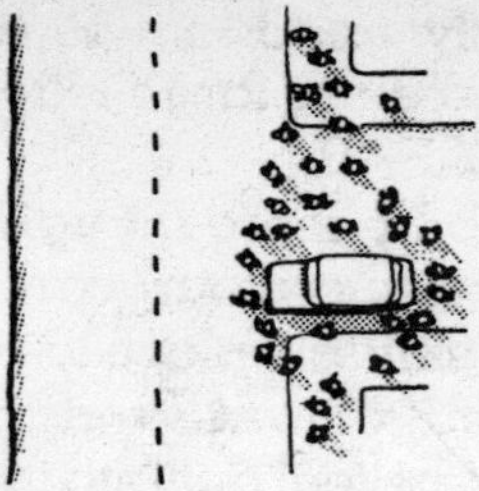

move to a Zebra crossing – literally – by religiously staying behind the car in front in slow-moving traffic. When he stops just past a Zebra crossing you quickly move up to fill the gap, leaving yourself straddled across the crossing while the irate pedestrians have to squeeze through the six-inch space between his rear bumper and your bonnet.

Now apply the same principle to other cars, especially when there's a stream of cars waiting to come out of a side road and the traffic in front of you stops just the other side of it:

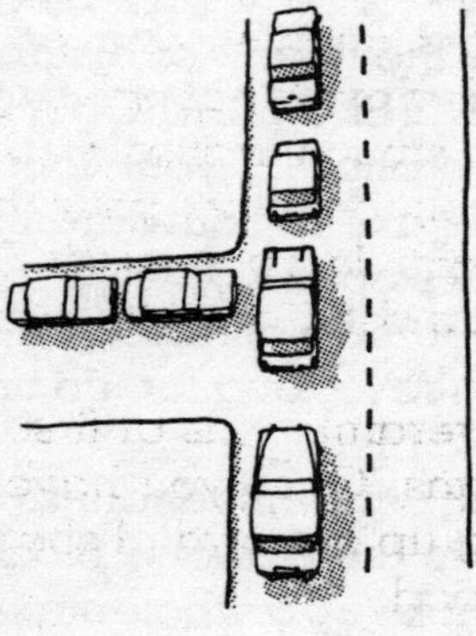

It is particularly important to apply this technique when there are large letters on your road saying KEEP CLEAR.

And do try to be more thoughtful when parking. Before leaving your car ask yourself if there's a more suitable place to park it – opposite another parked car in a narrow street, for example, or a few feet out into the road?

Then there's finding someone's house. When you have several impatient drivers behind you, slow down and start looking from side to side at the street names or house numbers. Every so often look as if you think you've found it by coming almost to a standstill until the car behind you thinks you've stopped and he starts to pull out to overtake. At which point you discover that it's not the street/house you wanted and, without looking in your mirror, you set off again.

This is one of those occasions where you can use your indicators to good effect. While you're looking, indicate left from time to time to show that you may – or may not – be going to stop at some time in the near – or distant – future. BUT KEEP ROLLING SLOWLY FORWARD. This adds to the exasperation of your followers who are itching to overtake you but daren't do so until you have actually stopped.

If by some remote chance you happen to find the place you're looking for, do **not** indicate. Just stop there and then.

With enough pig-headedness and insistence on your rights there is one blocking technique which can choke up a whole street and bring the traffic to a standstill for miles around. It calls for careful timing. Look for a spot in a narrow street where two vehicles are parked almost opposite each other – with the one on **your** side slightly further away – and there is a vehicle coming in the opposite direction who will need to pull out into your lane in order to get through:

Just as he is about to make this manoeuvre you quickly fill the gap. After all, it is **your** piece of road:

While you sit there glaring at each other a long line of traffic will build up behind him so that he can't reverse to let you through. And another line of traffic will build up behind **you** so that you can't reverse for him either . . . not that you would anyway:

It's an advanced roadpig's dream. Tens, hundreds, maybe even thousands of vehicles all jammed up and unable to move. And you have the satisfaction of knowing that you are completely in the right.

IN CASE YOU THOUGHT WE WERE JOKING . . .

Competition among roadpigs is intense and there must be many claimants to the title of Britain's Worst Driver. But few can match the achievements of the star in the following real-life drama.

It happened in a one-way street in a quiet shopping area of Thorpe Bay Broadway, Essex, at 2.30 on a Thursday afternoon. The police officer who had the unenviable task of trying to sort the whole thing out describes the incident in his own words:

There were cars parked on either side of the road and a large baker's van was double banked on the left-hand side. The driver of the baker's van got out and started to unload a number of wire baskets – the square type which you place on a small square trolley – and drag them off to a nearby shop. As the van driver entered the shop

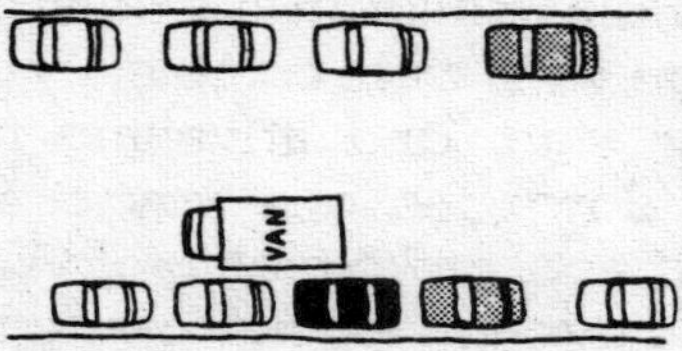

an 86-year-old man returned to his motor car, which was a Morris Oxford Automatic. Unfortunately, the van was now parked beside his car and he could not get out.

The driver of the vehicle immediately behind the Morris Oxford also returned and by using reverse was able to pull away from the kerb and drive off.

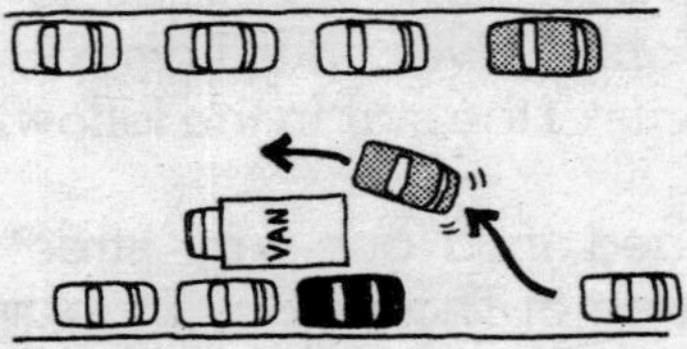

Almost at the same time, the driver of the Morris Oxford began to sound his hooter in an attempt to make someone move the bread van. The driver of the van heard the noise and walked out of the shop, towing behind him the trolley which was now laden with twelve empty wire baskets stacked one on top of the other. He began to gesture to the Morris Oxford driver, pointing to himself and then his van and then up the road, a signal which we would all understand. However, the Morris Oxford driver didn't see the van driver.

Meanwhile, a little further down the road, two more large vans were completely obscuring the 'No Entry' sign, and travelling in the wrong direction down the one-way street came the proud owner of a two-month-old Vauxhall Viva. He passed through the narrow gap between the stationary bread van and the stationary vehicles on the far side of the road.

Seated in his two-week old Wolseley 1300 on the right-hand side of the road, was a well-meaning motorist who began to flash his head-lights and wave his hands and sound his horn in an attempt to stop the Vauxhall driver proceeding further up the one-way street.

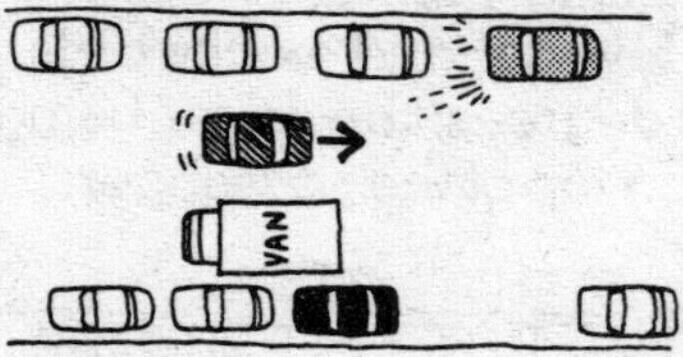

At the same time the driver of the Morris Oxford looked round and saw the now vacant spot behind his car. He quickly engaged reverse and at the same time applied pressure to the accelerator pedal. Being an automatic the response was quite frightening. The rear wheels actually spun on the road surface before the vehicle began to reverse.

At that precise moment, the driver of the Vauxhall, having realized his mistake, spotted the vacant gap behind the Morris Oxford and

pulled over to his right with his nose towards the kerb intending to reverse out and travel off in the direction whence he came.

He had just reached the stationary position when the Morris Oxford rocketed backwards, the Morris driver applying 'right-hand down', striking the Vauxhall Viva on the offside rear wing. This immediately solved the Vauxhall Viva's reversing problem because his car was pushed sideways and backwards through an angle of 45 degrees, the driver being thrown out of his seat on top of the passenger.

Undaunted, the Morris Oxford continued on in his curved path, now travelling at right angles to the flow of the traffic, and hit the side of the Wolseley 1300 with the amazed driver sitting watching what was going on.

The Wolseley was pressed hard against the kerb, and as it was a fairly deep kerb the car stopped, but the Morris Oxford was still travelling backwards and the entire nearside body compartment of the Wolseley began to fold inward. As the car could not travel to its side because of the kerb, and as pressure was still being applied by the driver of the Morris Oxford, the leverage caused both cars to lift slightly from the ground. This lifting effect released the pressure on the tyres of the Morris Oxford and the wheels began to rotate – although not completely off the ground. Large volumes of acrid smoke began to come from the tyres as the two vehicles hung there. The driver of the Wolseley was unable to get out of his vehicle and the driver of the Morris was unaware of what had happened. He then engaged Drive, causing him to hurtle forward.

In the meantime, the driver of the Vauxhall Viva had recomposed himself and opened his offside door and was muttering to himself 'What the . . .' when the door distintegrated around his hand as the Morris Oxford struck the Viva again and continued on. This impact caused a slight deviation in the steering of the Morris Oxford and was responsible for it striking the back of the bread van, a very severe blow which also demolished the front wing of the Morris and caused it to deviate slightly to its left. Fortunately for him, the driver of the bread van abandoned

his trolley load of cake trays because the Morris Oxford hurtled onto the footpath scattering the said trays in all directions.

Realizing that parking on the footpath is not permitted, the Morris Oxford driver quickly engaged reverse and with tyres smouldering, hurtled backwards again. This time he struck the Vauxhall Viva on the front side wing with the as yet undamaged nearside rear of the Morris Oxford. The Vauxhall Viva was pushed backwards across the road and fortunately the driver, in a state of panic, managed to apply the handbrake before colliding with vehicles on the far side of the road.

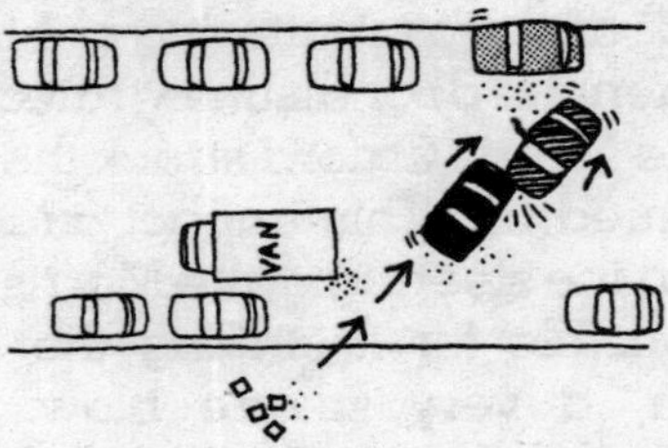

At this point a well-wisher leapt forward and snatched the ignition keys from the Morris Oxford which prevented any further too'ing and fro'ing across the road. The police were called and arrived very soon to find the driver of the Morris Oxford seated behind the wheel muttering 'the damn thing's broken down'. Having established nobody was hurt, the police then interviewed the driver of the Morris Oxford who was attempting to read the registration number which was mounted high up on the bread van.

The Morris driver was blaming everyone else for the accidents – the woman who drove out and left the space there, the van driver who double banked, the b . . . . . fool who flashed his lights – in fact, everyone apart from himself.

This incident had its conclusion in the local magistrates' court where the Morris Oxford driver was suspended from driving until he had passed his test. He had the cheek to take six driving lessons before finally giving up.

Courtesy of Frank Wilkin, Southend Police

SEND US YOUR FAVOURITE ROADPIG STORIES

No-one can drive for long without being made at some time to feel a complete and utter fool. And we all have our pet funny stories of the antics of all those **other** complete and utter fools.

If you want to see your favourite motoring anecdote in print send it in to Michael Bland, c/o Arrow Books Limited, 17–21 Conway Street, London W1P 6JD. If there is a sufficient response the best ones will be compiled into a 'Book of Great British Roadhogs' and the contributors of published items will be sent an autographed copy.